ADAM'S DREAM

PETER McDONALD

Adam's Dream

BLOODAXE BOOKS

ISBN: 1 85224 333 3

First published 1996 by
Bloodaxe Books Ltd,
P.O. Box 1SN,
Newcastle upon Tyne NE99 1SN.

Bloodaxe Books Ltd acknowledges
the financial assistance of Northern Arts.

AEF-7693

Cover printing by J. Thomson Colour Printers Ltd, Glasgow.

Printed in Great Britain by
Cromwell Press Ltd, Broughton Gifford, Melksham, Wiltshire.

for Howard Erskine-Hill

Acknowledgements

The poem 'D.G. Rossetti, *The Orchard Pit*' draws heavily upon 'The Orchard Pit', a prose fragment by Rossetti 'written with a view to the composition of a poem [...] towards 1871' according to W.M. Rossetti in his edition of *The Collected Works of Dante Gabriel Rossetti* (London, 1886). The text is found in Volume I, pp.427-30 of this edition.

In both the title-poem 'Adam's dream' and the series of poems making up part III of this collection, I am indebted to two books in particular relating to the eighteenth-century Scottish architect Robert Adam: James Lees-Milne's *The Age of Adam* (London, 1949), and John Fleming's *Robert Adam and his Circle in Edinburgh and Rome* (London, 1962). In 'Adam's dream', where Robert addresses his brother James, I have borrowed from a letter of 11 August 1758, written in fact to Alexander MacMillan (quoted in Lees-Milne, pp.24-25). The Lord Bute, referred to by Robert as 'our bold Scipio', did go on to exercise some powers of patronage in favour of the Adam family, though the decline in his political fortunes was to set a limit to this. Robert's various plans for the rebuilding of Lisbon in the wake of the earthquake of 1757 are discussed in Fleming's *Robert Adam and His Circle*; they came to nothing, and seem to have been at best half-serious. In these and other respects, I have allowed myself a number of historical liberties. The term 'Adamitic', although not noted as such in the second edition of the *Oxford English Dictionary*, seems to have been in use in the eighteenth century to describe Adam style; Sir John Soane uses it also in his lectures to the Royal Academy, delivered over the period 1809-36.

Some poems bear dedications to people who have been, wittingly or otherwise, instrumental in their composition: 'Bitter' is for Harry Smart; 'The creatures' for Howard Erskine-Hill; 'From the porch' for Boyd Johnson and Ayse Turksevan; and 'Delaval' for Jo Shapcott.

Acknowledgements are due to the editors of the following publications in which some of these poems first appeared: *gls/the big spoon*, *The Honest Ulsterman*, *Modern Irish Poetry* (Blackstaff Press, 1995), *Pivot* and *The Poetry Book Society Anthology 1* (PBS/Hutchinson, 1990). Some poems were also broadcast on Diversions (BBC Radio Ulster).

Contents

III

I

Flat sonnet: the situation

To speak exactly about the situation is difficult,
and yet to speak inexactly is unpardonable,
reshaping it at best as some half-blurred fable
where lines undraw themselves, boundaries move and halt,
the thing you see is never necessarily
the thing you see, and what happens there does not happen;
for the line undrawn draws the line, only to cheapen
what was dear-bought with its discreet bargaining.

Now the demand is that you deal with the situation
and come to the table with an answerable reply,
there is either warranted flatness or the clear lie
and between these, perhaps, a line kept at high tension
on which to balance or fall, a choice that draws you in
where there is no choice but to deal with the situation.

Meissen

Everything he touched, it fell to pieces:
small signs at first – the moth
whose wings just brushed his fingers
left them powdered with gold and silver,

with sharp dust scattered in a breath;
then the slightest pressure on a delicate page
would make it crumble, the least
gesture over a glass's edge

and the glass would cringe and crack.
Room by room, the house deformed
itself around him, the doors eased back
from their hinges, the wood split,

rafters and beams gave out and fell
to thick dust on dissolving carpets;
his hand, poised over the bannister,
would have suddenly nothing to cling to,

and his bare head, like a clown's,
whitened under a shower of plaster.
Each fresh collapse would bring through
patches of sky, vistas of clear air,

emptiness surprising him everywhere
in failures and quick breakdowns.
When the house was almost gone,
its gables fizzling into the sky,

only the precious things were left:
the cabinets of good porcelain,
Derby, Sèvres, Limoges, Meissen,
somehow outlasting all the rest,

and their militant fragility
defeated him, defeated now
his heavy house, his body,
his heavy solid hands;

they left him without the grounds
for touching, with all his needs astray,
not ruined quite or hurt, but somehow
reduced, and better that way.

On a good day

The shadow over your shoulder
looks down, and you can't look down

from out on the very edge
where a cubic pressure of air

crushes or lifts maybe
even you

drunk and beat-up and weary,
still balanced, a heavy

head that rests on nothing
and will fall

from the edge of anything,
a displaced volume

of a certain weight
pressured, pressed

as shame, emblem,
sweet liquor

where the shadow looks
down, and you can't look.

Reno

At noon, in the building that has no daylight,
a rider steps into his wire globe
– above us by twenty or twenty-five feet –
and starts up a glittery motorcycle,

then a woman in sequins and little else
stands still at one point in his orbit,
untouched forever, as he drives up
and around the world on the wrong side.

Endtime

The flat road with no corners and no end
will take you further on, in either direction,
into the state of Texas; even at night
this is hot ground, it should be glowing red,
but instead the franchises are lighting your way,
part-empty, cool, just waiting you quietly
whenever you come, and you come sometime.

The woman who was sitting a table away
looks older than anything reasonable or possible,
and now she is here beside me
she has shaken my elbow and wakened me
before I am put to the question;
she moves up a jar of pickled jalapeños
and blesses me three times in the name of Jesus.

She will ask me three things, and she will wait
for no answers (the answers are there in my heart):
do I have eyes to see the manifest signs?
do I walk each day in fear of eternity?
– and then, as she leaves her shining table
to move on towards the night and the heat –
do I believe we are living in endtime?

Slumped on a low wall, out in the dark here
on the loud far edge of the parking-lot,
too tired for driving, too tired for anything,
you might as well be in on the secret;
you might as well be caught out on your own
with no questions and no answers,
finished, in Texas someplace, waiting dawn.

Breakfast

I cut and press the five blood oranges
into a jug, and sit down by the window.

Maybe the runners see me for a moment,
somewhere out on the very edge of attention,

as I sit drinking the blood of the oranges –
a table and a glass, a heavy head.

(This is the touch of hands that weigh and balance
like someone blind, who could feel colours once,

and sits at the window with a glass of blood.)

Bitter

If they had names once, their names are not to be spoken
    without a shudder; if they had faces, their faces
are turned down now for good – forgotten, smeared things;
    nothing is left to distinguish one from another,
a row of bared heads, heavy with disgrace and dishonour.
    If there are words in which to remember their actions,
they will not form in the mouth, and a voice alone cannot bear them.

Exposed in sleep or drink, it may be that violence rises
    as a sharp, sour taste in the throat, or a tension
winding through muscles until it reaches some point of abandon:
    whatever it is takes shape in the dark, whatever
form or figure appears – some crouched, famished shadow
    with plastery hair and the stretched lips of an enemy –
the hands and will together consent in strength to its murder.

A line of men, each of whom will have done nothing or something,
    stand with heads bowed before their accusers,
each of whom will speak bitterness, and will use bitterness,
    until the hard tension passes, relief comes,
and at last the quiet shapes are laid to rest or abandoned.
    If there are victims, the victims are hard to distinguish
as taste from the tongue, the fist from the blow, or hands from the body.

The Brancusi room

As he stares at the peeled head
of Brancusi's *Prometheus*
(exactly still, resting on nothing)
the gallery reels around him;
he becomes an unfixed point
in the white room
where all possible dreams of falling
confirm themselves,
taunted, on the way down,
by *Bird in space*, its steadied leap
from here to there exactly.

It is afterwards, dizzied and shame-faced,
that his talk is of balance,
of precipices, chasms, headlong falls,
the leap of faith
involved in putting one foot out
in front of the other;
the story, to cap it all,
of the bicycle built for speed
he was given on his tenth birthday,
and which even now – look, look –
he cannot ride.

A hard place

Not everybody is happy, or loved:
despite that, at seven-thirty or thereabouts
this evening, some kids and some short-lived
breezes dawdled up here from the harbour,
all the way to the bar, and without
picking up, without placing an order
they left, slipped back into the heatwave,
      as if nobody had moved.

Even among the losing team
(heavy losers – one drinks, then cries some,
another mutters through old-time hymns
while his enemy half-sleeps on the table)
something comes loose, and maybe the rock seems
far enough from a hard place to let crumble,
like a sign slipping, or like some emblem:
      an emblem of suffering and shame?

The glen

There was a garden behind the labourers' cottage,
studded with white and blue, yellow and orange,
where waves of flowers and walls of trained roses
ran down a slope into grass, to the point
where shrubs and trim hedges marked a boundary;
beyond that, weeds and brambles, a tangle
of nettles and docken as the ground dropped
down finally into the glen. Trees spread over
the gap, and beneath them was darkness, the sound
of branches and leaves; sometimes, from underneath,
water invisibly going its own way.

So the boundary was a sheer edge, the slope a drop,
and the bright flowers had a shadow behind them
that could speak sometimes over brash colours
and mumble into the cottage's dry parlour
something fearful, or to do with sorrow,
a hard thing, extreme, just inches away
and unavoidable; no words, not an inch given,
but the glen still running behind everything,
always there at the end of a packed garden,
and me listening sometimes,
between us only the simple matter of falling.

There again

Reading in this sharp light above the clouds,
well-fed, one-quarter drunk, no children screaming,
I can imagine the many forms of my arrival,
all of them simple and sudden, from nowhere.

The creatures

At day's end, in a lull beneath stained and watery heavens,
    the beasts return in pairs to pace out the twilight
heavily, lightly: striped pigs, sad apes, the great lions,
    cattle and sheep, old bears, the hound and the badger,
creatures now without Adam to name or Noah to save them,
    coming back to a forest, a garden of calls and responses,
their eyes full of bleary light from skies full of water.

All around foliage moves in the air, making no progress
    this way or that; long vines, weighted branches
and outsized, flat leaves consort in wet tangles
    where birds rustle and screech, or where light animals
purposefully skelter, finding places to hide or to forage
    in a larger confusion of such ill-sorted species:
the coconut, the mangrove, the elm, the pine and the chestnut.

A red sun gutters here, as if at the point of exhaustion,
    from some far place, one beyond all purpose and action;
the moon comes; now insects flash up unknowable signals
    while lonely calls, like grief, go out in the darkness:
they echo each other, concluding that all has been done now,
    and all is to do again, for the creatures are leaving;
one by one, and with sorrow, they must enter the peaceable kingdom.

Peacetime

Half-way down you lose the sense of falling,
call off hostilities between things and the soul
and wave perhaps, now time is to spare,
on the clear road from here to wherever;
for everyone is crying in relief
and congratulation, historians and survivors
discuss their grievous memories on air,
dizzy in this late reprieve and freedom,
and it all hurts like a childbirth, crazy
with drugs and news and people and champagne.

This is all happening before its time
or after; this is weekend leave;
these are the experts and the blonde children
ready to sing, like a happy army;
this is a good day for flying;
this is the cat's-
cradle of the bridge and the excellent sky;
this is the safe end of everything;
this is the beard and the dropping
smile of John Berryman going to heaven.

Five circumstances

There is a sad place, where everything is resolved.
The people smile there, but out of politeness,
and look forward to their time off-duty
which will not come. They consider this, also.

*

Having arrived at the point of utter exhaustion,
you must face the point of abandon, face up
to the point of despair, as to the last point
of land before the ocean: this is the point.

*

This is the man who has failed in everything
but wakes up happy to greet the world.
As the cat bounds into the filthy yard
he senses his good wishes being returned.

*

A packed room tenses as the conversation
holds up to wait for the decisive moment
when a man will announce in perfect English,
and with regret, that the conversations are ending.

*

It is like travelling with sorrow everywhere:
the business suit pressed but showing its age;
a newspaper folded in on the bad news;
a briefcase full of tears and pornography.

From the porch

If you sat here long enough,
not any long time, but for lifetimes,
for the centuries without you,
then into your death and beyond it
in a moment, the space of a breath,
you would see just about everything:
colours on the sierras coming
and going, fires and black scars
for miles, then sudden regrowths,
years of pitiless summers
that beat this ground, snows freezing it,
all the generations of birds
circling and unidentifiable;
the passing hunters who squat
over worn stones, their voices
gone as you take a breath;
the hillsides opened by water,
the men who came for gold
and left without it, Chinese
workers camping out, soon gone,
and then, in the blink of an instant,
in half a breath, in less,
ourselves here watching and waiting,
who are gone just as quickly
to be followed, it seems, by everything:
noise and a blur of crowds
then a sudden silence,
but one that's broken maybe,
like the quiet behind our sleep
when a dog nudges at the trash
or two cats scramble into each other,
and sounds start to rise and fall,
like breath at night coming and going,
of the tall horses moving uneasily,
or deer that came in close at dusk,
the roosting birds, the sharp lizards,
the hare or the jack-rabbit
all following their noses,
like lost things.

An eclipse

I walked home in the dark and beneath trees
that cried and scraped above me as they strained
to keep themselves together in the wind;
      a solid month of storms,
         drunken calamities
that came to nothing, the weather on bad terms
with everyone, picking fights, ready to wound,
      earnest of proper harm.

I walked back safe under the cracking branches
as fists of air pummelled and slapped me hard
for some good reason, as yet undeclared;
      I felt glad and light-headed
        to be in the clutches
of a gale that could break whole trees unaided,
yelling and stamping, head down, undeterred,
      something tensed and decided.

I spoke across three thousand miles of weather,
drunk and exhausted, to you wide awake;
my closing time darkened your six o'clock
      with half-unspoken anger
        – a shadow, rather,
of something big, to be appeased like hunger,
beyond us, and on which we cannot look,
      some close and awful stranger.

I woke up with the storm still in my head
and damage spread for acres, shattered wood
exposed and almost white across the road;
      I sat on the cold stairs,
        I ran and hid
to find myself naked, as if behind bars,
still grey with shadows, blurting out proud
      sobs and baby tears.

I went outside tonight, again let loose,
where pieces of wood still clutter up the path,
to wait for the eclipse (for what that's worth –
        a sight for lovers, who kiss
            and cry in twos),
and standing on my own, watched the moon pass
into a coloured shadow of the earth
        pardoned, and numb with peace.

The passions

Being obliged to climb higher, there is nothing else for it
but to try the steps, some solid, then one or two missing,
that cling to the inside wall; yet lichens and mosses

are at home on the worn stones where, slippy with drizzle,
your feet slide and catch hold; one final scramble
and you are out in the open, where weather is loud and the daylight

seems to come and go in gusts, brightening, darkening
that marginal road you drove along, the hills in the distance,
the new farmhouses, and out on a rainy horizon, the sea.

Yet even here, high up in a far place, you are scarcely
alone – just look: all around, behind you and beneath you,
there are the slow lines of raised, unreadable faces

which you must transform into figures expressing the passions
– rage, terror, pity, desire and ruinous sorrow –
and these are the very faces to see you through to the end,

all the way up, slipping and holding, climbing at last
to some high place half in ruins – a bridge or a tower,
but a bridge over nothing and a tower with no view from it –

until their perfect expressions are all wiped in an instant
and somebody – call it you – has to go down like a dummy
and measure an empty distance between here and the ground.

Delaval

'Here is Mr Dillyval, and a charming set of Glasses that sing like nightingales, and we have concerts every other night.'
THOMAS GRAY, TO WILLIAM MASON, 1761

Alone, where there is no etiquette to breach,
the hands may go free to toy with a napkin,
dismember gutted fruits, or wet the fingers
and edge them over one particular glass

until a note starts up and holds briefly,
clear, then fitful and guttering. May a note gutter?
It is later than midnight in the depleted Parlour,
yet the reflexes of taste still prick like nerves,

as if conscience would speak on behalf of decorum
and ask repentance for our every mistake
in the name of such fitness. At the sounded note
one flame does gutter; it is time indeed

to snuff the candles and leave the room to darkness.

*

How meagre the skill one has in this music!
How halting and imperfect, how much like a failure
seems even the recollection of Mr Dillyval
and his concerts *impromptu* on the musical glasses

that haunt the same room now, however faintly.
All evening, seated next to the contrivance,
he played, touching harmonics from the vessels
arranged by diameter, and for each note a colour,

melodies at an even pace, bright with echoes
that rang and repeated and circled themselves,
returning always to the placed intervals.
Often that season the company sat late

when there was much talk, and not without wit,
over the music or the manner of it,
ingenious improvements to the mechanism,
or the fit posture from which to touch the colours.

Although not wholly wasted on the air,
such sounds do not return, and a bell strikes
to mark the quarter-hour, just once.
The blood returns now to its slow course

and customary rhythms gather ground,
not troubled far by virtuosity,
nor shaken greatly by such memories
when the melodies themselves are past recall.

(Here is a small failure, and no consequence,
safe in the dark alone, returning homeward
on the familiar, unmistaken path
upstairs, the weary way.)

On show

There is, first, the disappointment of a case
around even this insured figurine:
you will stare for minutes, and more the next day,
until your sad amazement has grown routine,
at the face and the small body in porcelain,
her eyes that look through glass
as though towards you, to confirm beautifully
and for good the usual futilities:
the projects for love, like plans for money or knowledge,
shut away in a clear light, all of them frangible.

Academic sentences

1 *First principles*

This cannot be seen, and accordingly it is incapable of producing
the image you claim to see; it cannot be heard, in any useful or
commonly acceptable sense of the term, and so can hardly emit
those sounds you find so troubling; it cannot sustain itself on any-
thing other than the thin air of your imagination; you must allow
it therefore to die.

All of the buildings are empty, all of the men and women have
left them, and what remains is the focus principally for objective
interest, for the sorting and weighing of evidence; not certainly for
your hurt brooding, with its intrusions of desire and exaggeration,
both (frankly) vain and ridiculous, or the interruptions of insigni-
ficant deaths.

A grand project for nothing; visions, plans, lost patterns; two
worlds of life and death, involved only in an image of something
invisible: none of this counts, in the place where somehow you
must build solid structures on soft ground, whatever you choose
to understand by the word for clay, or reddened earth.

2 *Point A*

She lives now in an unbuilt project of the brothers Adam, among
purely notional fitments and decorative schemes, prepared, at any
and every moment, to go public with this odd address, this mau-
soleum, to christen it Point A and perhaps, should it prove neces-
sary, herself sell tickets at the door.

Even with its glories on show, certain secrecies involved in the
building will probably remain obscure: tiny letters, from Alpha to
Omega, worked into the stones of the main staircase; arcane pat-
terns on the tiles inside one particular fireplace; a frieze high over
the entrance bearing signs of the sun and stars.

Her eye for detail is exact and terrifying, involving as it does the recognition of thousands of points of error or of neglect, architectural white lies accepted in the course of things but which, if she comes into the house, she must put right, moving from room to room and restoring all she finds.

3 *Eidolon*

I am not speaking at all now, although I am surrounded as I sit here by moving blocks of silence and bad sound; there are lights and noises that make their way to me from the night outside, and there is my own slumped figure reflected, facing me but with the fast lights inside it, spread across the window.

I would ask things of this image, I would interrogate it with an impressive thoroughness and integrity, if there were a possibility of its answering my questions; the image would reply – candidly, shamefully, stricken – if there were really a chance of my questioning it aloud: but neither I nor the image must speak a syllable here.

The image is a shadow with features; my features are shadowed horribly over its face, the clear surfaces and the parts that recede into darkness: pierced by roadlamps and headlights, the likeness ghosts itself, it negotiates hopelessly between two sleeping partners, between the heat of bodies and the kindcold sky.

4 *Walking in the garden*

Although the ground is level and the path clear, I could be walking a wire as I speak to her, beginning to fall in one direction and then beginning to fall in another, teetering steadily, balanced and terrified, talking about nothing at all with my head straight up and looking forwards.

As she turns off the marked path, towards the slab of architecture and the black open doorway that leads straight into its heart, I call her back on some pretext, seeing already a prospect of ruins, vistas of pure waste, smashed marble, unpeopled wreckage, Babylon, dust.

And she answers, but what she says is unbearable, it cannot be faced and has to be forgotten; she fills my shadow and moves from A to B, from B to A, speaking about choices beyond my making, touching the laden apple-tree and laughing, whether at me or herself it is impossible to tell.

5 *B*

After so many drawings, so many outlines sketched in pencil, scrubbed and redrawn, and later whole designs inked meticulously on sheets of heavy paper, after so many walls and windows, porticos and pilasters appearing, shifting, vanishing sometimes, after all these exertions, these artful comings and goings, the mind and the hand rested together.

The grand project (B, for ease of reference) exists therefore (if 'exists' is the appropriate word) in multiple states, some of them conjectural, its development and interruptions, the conceptual leaps and the digressions hard to distinguish, just as it is debatable, finally, whether the building is located in imagination or in memory.

(False starts and premature endings, losses and conjectures, someone listening to a piano with her face turned always half away, deep in a house where all the doors are closed, a figure remembered or imagined, but subtracted, its name going in the fire, and now scorched almost away.)

The glass harmonica

Now it starts:
the music being played on glasses,
'unearthly', echoing itself, up in the air,
dividing into separate, ringing parts
that make feints and passes
at each other like a courting pair
alone, together, alone,
sounding the resonance of one another's hearts.

(But of this world all along:
that these had grown
above themselves, were wrong
and overblown
parts of a voiceless song,
is easily shown.)

Like a tulip-bud
the smallest glass, the highest note,
is lead-painted with the rest in its own shade,
and of all the *virtuosi* in the flood
of players who had by rote
each composition, the last has played
his last, and waits alone
in quiet now, with all the music in his blood.

About Lisbon

Now the city is almost completely empty,
the night is far through, with no moon, just stars;
a dog maybe scrambles in and out of the rubbish
along a side-street of no real interest or merit:
it's as if the whole place is ready to be erased
and somehow somebody has told the inhabitants.
Late as it is, there ought surely to be people
to find their way around the city of Lisbon
and guide me, who am not here, to the very spot
where the public clock stopped on a Sunday
and the tremors began. Is it perhaps because
that morning has yet to come, or because
the catastrophe has been too long forgotten
that nobody speaks, that there is nobody to speak,
that I must wander for hours an unknown city
and there is nobody here to ask the time?

The earthquake

A row of figures on the mantel, not yet of any particular value,
  begin to tremble and burr, edging their way to the edge.

Scintillant dusk: outside, an unmistakable hue and commotion
  of falling things, panic, after-the-fact calls of alarm.

The shepherdess has just taken the plunge with her pastoral lover
  and gone off into shards and smithers, to smithereens.

II

D.G. Rossetti, *The Orchard Pit*

Yes, it begins in a dark place – it does of course –
as lights come towards me from that clinging darkness
resembling faces, or finally just the one face,
refined away from accidents by death,
therefore distinct at last from everything human,
and stranger than in life, its hair a flaming corona,
the blue eyes beyond change and set for ever,
the lips fuller now, stark on its pale features.

Men will tell you this is a common enough dream,
yet it seems to be the only dream I have,
or have had, for as long as I remember:
the dark place is a glen whose sides slope upward
from the bed of a stream that has almost dried away,
and either slope is covered up completely
with apple trees, scores of wild apple trees.
She is standing in a fork between the limbs
of the largest tree, singing, stretching one arm
along a branch, while with the other she holds
out a red apple for some passer-by.
Beneath her feet, the thick roots tangle down
and tug until they stretch from side to side
across the gap they cover, the orchard pit:
that place is full of bodies, of men's bodies,
who lie in heaps beneath the screen of boughs,
each one with a bitten apple in his hand.
She is standing above their corpses and singing,
and sings for ever, and offers her apple still.
For me, this is no strange place: I know the glen,
I have known it always, and go there often now,
seeing nothing odd, but with a sense of words
half-heard, unknown, or (it may be) forgotten,
sharpening for me invisibly in the leaves,
as if this place were chosen for my grave.
Or what I barely hear forms into music,
a strange song without words or distinct lines,
making me think of the poems I might offer her,
as I take her voice, with its soft cadences,
into myself to give it shape and purpose,

until I know the song as I know the dell,
somewhere I might always have been from childhood.
Yet at night, when the evil dream itself returns,
her singing is painful and remote as ever,
and I cannot speak those words, if they are words,
which she sings from the fork in the apple tree.

How many men sleep in the covered pit?
There could be dozens of strangers lying there,
the young men she has had, the fathers of young men,
lovers who brushed against her, and fell headlong,
and those who worshipped her, and broke their hearts
for love, or what they called love, a huge need
for which there were no words except the sounds
her singing bodied into the tight evenings,
and which I hear now, and cannot stop hearing,
until I meet those men, and lie down with them:
though strangers, we shall know each other there,
when it will be too late for everything.
Already there seems to be no place of shelter,
nowhere at all safe from some premonition,
no peace to cover up the violent want,
for she is everywhere, and waiting for me
even as I sit down to speak of love
in comfort, with the woman who loves me.
I am surrounded by tenderness and trust,
so much so that she almost makes a joke
out of these things that she knows trouble me:
at table, I am offered a red apple
and my love questions me, though with kind laughter,
on why I am slow to take the Siren's fruit.
I must smile also, but when I cut the apple,
there at the centre, as if to mock us both,
a red stain spreads out like the stain of lips,
and its taste is bitter, then vivid and desperate
as a last kiss, or a first kiss. Do I betray her,
when she dares me to betray myself to her?
Another time, she leads me down the path
to the glen and to the apple trees in fruit:
she stands beneath one, plucks an apple for me,
and holds it out, and smiles. Then something snags,
she says she can hear voices in the boughs

calling for me, leaves muttering my name.
She hurls the apple out into the dell
and down it goes, far through the mesh of branches,
to the hidden place itself, deep underneath.
No laughter now, but a kind of sulky fear
as she asks me again, perhaps for the hundredth time,
to say that I love her, and will always love her:
the truth is that I love her as a stone
clattering down some frothy, gulping river
loves the stray leaf that clings to it in the foam,
and will vanish in a plunging swirl at last,
while the stone will sink and settle in the cold.
Just so, she wraps herself around me now
and gives me worried tears, and scared, sharp kisses.

Here is the truth: tonight, at last, I dreamed
how the end will come, for I not only saw,
in sleep, the lifelong pageant of the glen,
but I took my proper part in it, at last,
and learned for certain why that dream was mine.
I saw myself shambling towards the glen
and heard my love pleading with me to return,
yet I walked on until we stood together
on the very edge, with the trees moving beneath us.
The moon, clear of some grey and scraggy clouds,
shone much too brightly, almost like thin sunlight,
giving the scene a cruel vividness;
she looked at me full face, and the tiny flaws
in her features, with the first few signs of age,
were evident and simple then as her grief,
without tears now, abandoned and appalled,
watching me go away from her, beyond her,
through an unquiet and hard-hearted distance
of leaves and blossom, branches and cold fruit
in which there waited, as she had always known,
the Siren I would discover at the last.
For the first time, I could hear words in the singing
that came from somewhere high up in the trees:
three verses, each one stretched impossibly
over and across the half-familiar music,
while the words were flat and obvious, purloined
from third-rate sentimental balladry:

the first refrain was *Come to me, come to love,*
a second followed, *Come to me, come to life,*
the third – predictably – was *Come to death;*
it was as if something had come back cheapened.
Despite the faint release of disappointment
I pressed on, knowing all that was to come,
and ready to fall down. So then I saw her,
saw first the light her hair made in the shadows
as the moon struck reds and golds and flashing ambers
around her face and shoulders, her bare neck
where a single ruby glowed like a fresh wound;
her delicate cold breasts, the eyes themselves,
alert to nurture or destroy, looked at me
while she held the apple inches from my face.
What could I do but take it? At that moment
I kissed her, or she kissed me – our lips touched –
and her hair fell down like rain over my eyes.
I lost my footing then, and dropped at once
through roots and scrambly undergrowth, my hand
still holding the bitten apple, to crash flat
into a mess of bodies, none of them moving,
unable myself to move a single muscle.
At last then, I was lying among my own,
and woke, as a man who has been close to death
wakes unafraid, part of him gone already,
with a woman's hair beside him on the pillow,
over his face, threading his cheeks and forehead,
crossing his eyelids, crossing his dry lips.

The hands of Juan Perón

It was going to take four of us at least:
one to kill the floodlights and blind
the cameras whirring at their posts,
another to slip out from behind
the thick-set line of trees and past
the guards' hut, moving from lock to lock
with the quick fingers of a surgeon;
then, and this is where I came in,
for dragging the lead far enough back
from the roof of his bunker coffin,
the services of two or three strong men.

They had set the date for early June,
mentioning things like a rising curve,
a jump in the temperature, tides
having to be taken on the turn;
knowing they would have reasons of their own
as well as reputations to preserve,
all I could do was set a modest price
and say that a poor man sees both sides
no matter what the question;
I told them I never ignored advice,
and yes, I'd always forget a face.

The night when it came was thick with heat,
settled alike over moonless slums
and the new road, lighted and straight,
that led to the gates and the big trees
swaying at the edge of his estate.
Even here, there was the city noise
and insects, and faint clicks and hums
that came from the gateman's intercom;
beneath us, twigs and gravel gave
the tiniest hints of our presence;
just after midnight, we made our move.

Everything was happening at long distance;
there were maybe fifty or sixty yards
between me and that mausoleum
(a wedding-cake in black marble,
swollen up solid with importance),
as I watched the first of two guards
go down, and one man sidle
up to the locked door of the tomb:
he knelt there like a pilgrim
for a matter of seconds, then gave the sign
to bring us out into the open.

Just like in dreams where you run for miles
uphill, towards or away from something,
we were up and into the dead hall
with its musty drapes and flags, its tiles
running cold beneath us all along
the polished path to his resting place.
We climbed the casket like a wall:
a tiny spotlamp had been left on
for a nightlight, and as we looked down
we saw him lying where it shone,
a child in bed, with a waxy face.

From behind us there were shouted whispers,
and a toolbag slung up and caught;
I was pulling him out by the epaulettes,
until his stuffed body with its taut
dried skin, its coiffure and powdered whiskers,
was sitting straight again; I brought
the two hands up from underneath
the lid; they were stained from cigarettes
but otherwise clean, stone-dry and brittle.
I blew, and chemicals under my breath
rose, then fell, as dust might settle.

The hacksaw was out and into his wrist
that minute, rasping its way through flesh
as though it had been dry paper; the rest
was simple, snapping bones like chalk,
then whipping his light hand off in a flash
and into a cushioned box; the right hand first
and then the left, the two laid flush,
wrapped over, and the lid jammed on.
We disappeared without needing to talk,
going our own ways, one by one,
taking with us the hands of Juan Perón.

Before we left I handed over a box
to the silent men who had stood behind me
watching, refining whatever their plans were,
too subtle to notice a simple hoax,
which is what I gave them. I'm holed up here
in this single room where they couldn't find me,
waiting until the right moment lands
like a dove with an idea in its beak
to put me in the money. So now, inside the Ark,
I'm left with the main chance, food for a week,
a telephone, and a clean pair of hands.

Adam's dream

It was the first morning after the earthquake:
imagine, Jamie, that prospect of desolation!
Everywhere, figures such as mine were moving
like ants among the remnants of pointless mazes,
dodging fires that burned on in the daylight
and structures liable still to collapse about them,
though searching really for the dead, one supposes,
the thousands of souls buried all together
in Lisbon that Sunday morning. I am not idle
Jamie, even in the few sultry hours
of sleep allowed me by this Roman weather,
and as I dreamed of the Portuguese disaster
I was starting to discern, in those very ruins,
the bold lines and the curves, the sweeps and contours
of a city to replace the shaken quarters,
laid out by me, and plotted in each detail
to accord with precept, principle, and good practice
in the antique taste which I have so well mastered
and of which you are, I know, an eager student.
(Of course, no more than you have I seen Lisbon,
but given such accounts of the devastation
it seems the place is fairly a *tabula rasa*
for a fellow of gifts and genius to work on.)

Think of it, to raise the Adamitic city!
I have listened to the invaluable Clérisseau
as he tutors me in figures of a morning,
repeating Voltaire's wisdom on the subject,
that Providence is under grave suspicion
for allowing such catastrophes to happen:
nonsense, the thing is plainly Heaven's judgement
intended for my behalf – do not you see it?
And the city to replace that shattered Lisbon
will be a wonder to the world of the discerning,
displaying to all Europe one true fashion
of the best taste, and flights of studied daring,
to trumpet my resource, my infinite merit,
and so become the first of Adam's cities.
Who knows, Jamie, but that you might be my partner
in building even London from its ruins?

As much as skill, good offices are needed
from men of rank, whose tastes we must encourage,
as best we can these days, with good example
and now and again, of course, judicious puffing:
one may not win that merited preferment
without a word or two in the right quarters,
and even here in Rome I have been active
in winning the good esteem of noble patrons
(not patrons yet, but like to be for someone),
and I take care that my name spreads through the city
as a likely man for great things in the future.
You recall I have written before of Piranesi
whose work bearing the handsome dedication
you will have received by now in a fine binding,
Antichità romane, the Roman matter
put over with great art, and greater detail
– which gives you, Jamie, solid ground for study.
This Piranesi is known to sing my praises
where weight is given to his good opinion,
so I have ample reason to be hopeful.
To see the antique world as you should see it,
ruined, but with the ruins free of clutter,
exposed as an ordered prospect of grand damage,
with here and there inconsequential figures
caught still as they go scuttling through the columns
is just what Piranesi seems to manage
in those etchings that have been my constant wonder
since I came here to Rome, this half-empty city.

In fact, it was the *Antichità* in folio
which featured in my dream about the earthquake:
not just the labyrinths of brick and *tufa*
half-grown with weeds, or the great dark masses
of drops and shadows, walls going on forever,
which I transposed from Rome into old Lisbon,
but the books themselves, the four bound volumes
which, you remember, Bute had desired of me
all of three months ago. Now, the bold Scipio
– without so much as a gesture of acquaintance,
a casual word of favour or approbation,
which would count for much, and very well repay me –
has sent the volumes back with a cold *thank you*,
as though I might have furnished them on approval

for his Lordship like a humble bookseller,
not a free Scot of generous means, and genius!
I shall be revenged on Bute, one way or other,
perhaps exactly as last night I dreamt it:
at Kensington, I'll wait for him on the bridge there,
while his barge progresses slowly down the river,
with him and *Madame la Princesse* busy as usual,
the Princess of Wales and her First Minister
stewing together through an English summer
(and causing the vessel some distress already
by their exertions, it being far from sturdy).
Under the bridge they'll come, like two locked wrestlers,
for me to let drop all four hefty volumes
on to the brilliant couple *in flagrante*
as they pass under the yoke and Robert Adam,
and send them down into the dirty water:
I'll fell Bute dead with the same Piranesi.

When Clérisseau arrived this morning, bedraggled,
(where had he lodged, I wonder? had he slept even?)
I put figures aside, and openly spoke with him
of the earthquake, of the plans of the Almighty,
of Piranesi, darkness, and Bute's exposed *derrière*.
We agreed this was a dream of injured merit,
a portent maybe, though confused and inscrutable,
of the great things we may expect in this world:
is it to be our lot, however deserving,
to be shadowed always, to be accidental figures
among the intransigent, huge forms?
                                    Jamie,
I believe the heat of Rome may bring me fevers
for which no remedy exists but work,
so commending that to you, in very good spirits
(at the door is news of another invitation),
I return now to take up my graceful labours.

III

'An IMAGE (in the most strict signification of the word) is the Resemblance of some thing visible: In which sense the Phantasticall Formes, Apparitions, or Seemings of visible Bodies to the Sight, are onely *Images*; such as are the Shew of a man, or other thing in the Water, by Reflexion, or Refraction; or of the Sun, or Stars by Direct Vision in the Air; which are nothing reall in the things seen, nor in the place where they seem to bee; nor are their magnitudes and figures the same with that of the object; but changeable, by the variation of the organs of Sight, or by glasses; and are present oftentimes in our Imagination, and in our Dreams, when the object is absent; or changed into other colours, and shapes, as things that depend onely upon the Fancy. And these are the Images which are originally and most properly called *Ideas*, and IDOLS, and derived from the language of the Graecians, with whom the word Εἰδω signifieth to *See*. They are also called PHANTASMES, which is in the same language, *Apparitions*. And from these Images it is that one of the faculties of mans Nature, is called the *Imagination*. And from hence it is manifest, that there neither is, nor can bee any Image made of a thing Invisible.'

THOMAS HOBBES: *Leviathan*

De gustibus

A bitter taste, and the tongue constrained always in the mouth;
candles at midday; a Scottish damp and the reek of mildew;
a painted room blistered and spoiled; the pattering of a moth
all day confronting smeary panes of the same window;
baronial vistas of unworked and waterlogged ground
into which the house itself begins surely to subside;
locked out of the way somewhere, plate tarnishing to the sound
of scraped, raw voices: soon everything will have to be denied.

Beyond this, an entire geography of ruin,
of ancient things brought down and broken to fragments,
restructures silently the half-darkness and rain
to clear and balanced forms; a light from the south brings
hope to the woodwormy desk, the card table in segments,
cracked delftware, the brutish glass and inkstand: tasteless things.

The authorities

It is true: knowledge is indeed matter for advancement
(Robert alone one morning with a volume of antiquities),
and principles of taste well founded on those sureties
from ancient practice will not lack proper emolument.
For each design one can imagine some enhancement,
but to rid the outlines of whatever superfluities,
to chasten style in a stern purging of impurities,
will expose an essential form, the severe monument.

Yet the monumental alone will not answer to taste;
one must make account first for the domestic fashion
that endures for the moment: light fluency and grace,
gaiety even – not the under-message of the authorities
(think of Spalato, the huge palace of Diocletian,
like all Dalmatia falling continually into ruin).

A pause

We are close now, it may be, to the delicate matter
which requires to be touched gently, if touched upon,
and for which all reserves of forethought and compassion
must lie ready to hand; neither to hurt nor flatter,
neither to let pass falsehoods nor to dissimulate,
and yet allow the substance to make itself apparent –
these are the special tactics of reserve and restraint
for which, and in which, patience is (so to speak) infinite.

The hesitation must arise from discomfort, even from pain,
a pause both taken and given; what will then emerge
may not in all decency be spoken of as yet,
although you may infer that its outline is sufficiently plain:
the imagination has enough here upon which to enlarge
in a quiet moment, and with such tact as it sees fit.

The rival

It is not genius at all: rather, a certain fertility
conjoined with application, and with luck perhaps,
which takes him far, striking the occasional felicity
in the course of things, but not daring to lapse
from the dull idiom for which he is praised so,
each project merely a serviceable facsimile
of something genuine, not his, and long ago
perfected, but refined now to a lucrative futility.

This is not complaint, but philosophy: if his public is deluded
in applauding him and rewarding him, little is proven;
one's own merit, infinite merit, might be given
hot praise as readily as indifference or blame,
and still it would remain to amend the taste of the time
regardless of all – promise, eminence, genius included.

The dedication

When Piranesi scrubbed the plate clean of its dedication
(to whom, out of discretion, let us not specify),
it was not towards any *milord* of the English nation
that *Roman Antiquities* now cast a flattering eye
but to ROBERT ADAM, ARCHITECT, the inscription
entered there like proper Latin, its own antiquity
amply attested by the cracked and weathered stone
on which the master spelt out his new dedicatee.

Robert's name, imagined in a garden of worn granite,
is therefore at once novel and enormously aged,
an artist's name preserved in the work of an artisan
(and all of this itself art, a graceful conceit),
so that nothing is old, or new, entirely: thus privileged,
he is heir to the name and title of an ENGLISHMAN.

In the sketchbook

Page upon page of the abandoned and the lost,
ideas without commission, flourishes, or gestures simply;
they crowd in from nowhere as if to build a new city
which is always beginning and cannot ever be finished,
for the first line drawn already imagines its parallel,
its perpendicular supports, and then embellishments,
the patterns that may be summoned in an instant,
accepted or rejected, found wanting or judged well.

This city is, naturally, without any inhabitants:
there is no room, and besides the dangers are great;
they will not suffer when finally the buildings are razed,
when the flat façades and the disproportioned pediments
crease and collapse into each other, and the crazed
architecture folds compactly into the stuff of light.

The aftermath

One by one, without show, and almost meticulously,
from underneath the splintered and multicoloured rubble
everybody emerged, all of the broken and innocent dead,
into a morning hazy with mizzle and lingering smoke
to dust themselves down and take stock of the catastrophe,
adrift suddenly in this new architecture of chaos
but able to recognise each other beneath masks of ash
and tear-lines, with open astounded eyes, bewildered
by movement again, the turns and surprises of their raised bodies.

Pious reflections

Brethren, just for one moment imagine them,
try to see them, however briefly, however faintly:
remote now from us and from our sadnesses,
their bones unbroken and their sore wounds healed,
they move in companies as the stars move,
in time to those celestial harmonies
which in these shadows are beyond us always,
and leave us just unblinded by their glory −

their clear eyes proof for ever against woe,
their music which encircles us for ever,
their flesh which is this common flesh no longer
but is changed now to the very substance of light −
brethren, just for this moment imagine them,
and seeing this, and hearing this, bear witness.

In his place

Maps on tables are charts of losses, ruin;
plotting vistas no longer there, he stumbles
over mazes of stone and marble turned to
pebbles, marks in the ground, sand, scrubby grasses.
Nearly finished, he sees the city rising
clear in front of his body, holding steady,
almost tangible, moving, breathing even,
so that stone is not stone, but white and fleshy
tissue, beaten and dense with living substance.
Carried out of such places, he imagines
cities bodied in airy, cold perspectives,
sees himself for a second their dim figment
raised in error among the classic orders
(poise, and even at great height, level balance),
figured simply for scale between the buildings.

Lines on the demolition of the *Adelphi*, 1937

Reader, I am the ghost of Robert Adam,
Come from the purgatory of the proud
To a London of headlights, fumes, and tarmacadam
Where these old buildings have been disallowed

As fusty relics in the way of things,
To watch the terrace fall, and wince again
While down the curious equipment brings
Investments once already down the drain

(Though now, indeed, the losses are not mine,
And I have pains other than injured pride
To see me through the ruins, for no design
Gives comfort in the place where I abide),

Yet I can see, beneath the sooty dust,
Nothing of lasting worth, no second Rome,
Merely an English place, mean, gone to rust,
Not, after all, the imagination's home,

And built on little more than unpaid debts,
Its future mortgaged and its past resigned,
No better than where Piranesi sweats
Beside me in the prison he designed.